AN IMPENDING RUPTURE OF THE BELLY

Matt Pelfrey

BROADWAY PLAY PUBLISHING INC
New York
www.broadwayplaypublishing.com
info@broadwayplaypublishing.com

AN IMPENDING RUPTURE OF THE BELLY
© Copyright 2007 by Matt Pelfrey

Cover image by Eric Pargac
First printing: December 2007
I S B N: 978-0-88145-360-7

Book design: Marie Donovan
Word processing: Microsoft Word
Typographic controls: Ventura Publisher
Typeface: Palatino

CHARACTERS & SETTING

CLAY STILTS, *thirties*
TERRI STILTS, *twenty-nine*, CLAY's *wife*
RAY STILTS, *thirties*, CLAY's *older brother*
EUGENE, *thirties*, CLAY's *co-worker*
DOUG, *thirty-forty*
ADAM
THE PRISONER

Time: Now

Place: Various locations suggested in the most minimal way.

Action should be continuous.

NOTE

The staging of the PRISONER is entirely up to the
director. He can be on stage from the moment of
his first appearance, lurking in his own space, or
he can exist only during scene transition, haunting
CLAY until the climax. Whatever seems organic to
the production and is most effective. Also, having an
intermission is completely optional. There was no break
in the world premiere.

AN IMPENDING RUPTURE OF THE BELLY received its world premiere on 7 April 2007 by the Furious Theater Company, artists-in-residence at the Pasadena Playhouse. The cast and creative contributors were:

CLAY STILTS .... Eric Pargac
TERRI STILTS .... Aubrey Saverino
RAY STILTS ....Shawn Lee
EUGENE/ADAM .... Doug Newell
DOUG/THE PRISONER .... Troy Metcalf

Director .... Dámaso Rodriguez
Sets ....Dan Jenkins
Costumes .... Christy M Hauptman
Lights ....Christie Wright
Sound .... Cricket S Meyers
Fight choreographer .... Brian Danner

for Alicia Pelfrey

ACT ONE

Scene 1

(CLAY *in a chair, isolated by a cold spear of light. A deep, aggressive voice speaks to him from the darkness.*)

MAN: Here's the thing: Out there, right outside, all the people driving by, stumbling to their lunch dates, plugged into their little phone gizmos—they're blind. They're ants. Not a clue. They read the paper and get teary about two-hundred-thousand just got wiped out by some horrific natural disaster. But they don't make the connection. The link. To their own lives. They don't honestly think it could happen to them. It's sad, screaming television people. Not anyone they know. They live in a fantasy land where the nightmares on T V stay on T V. But if it happens, they will crumble. They will be cut down in the street because living means standing your ground. And most can't. (*Beat*) So I guess my only real question for you, Clay, is: Do You Have What It Takes?

CLAY: Do I...?

(*The* MAN *appears, ominous, lurking on the edge of the light.*)

MAN: Can you do what has to be done?

CLAY: I think so.

MAN: Not good enough.

CLAY: I'm prepared to defend my family.

MAN: You're in a Ralph's. Looters've stripped the shelves bare 'cept for a lone loaf of wonder bread. An old woman grabs it before you. Respond.

CLAY: I...I guess I'd—

MAN: Guessing doesn't cut it. Your children haven't eaten for days! *Respond.*

CLAY: I take it.

MAN: She fights.

CLAY: I overpower her. She's just an—

MAN: She pulls a gun.

CLAY: Exactly how old is this woman? I mean—

MAN: Respond! I'm not playing games here. *She pulls a gun.*

CLAY: I...pull my gun?

MAN: And?

CLAY: I, uh, shoot her?

MAN: Do you?

CLAY: Yes.

MAN: An *old woman*?

CLAY: Yes.

MAN: Looks like your *grandmother*.

CLAY: I shoot her. Right between the eyes. I put her down.

(Beat)

MAN: And a cop? *(Off* CLAY's *silence)* Think the Police will be your friend when it happens? Huh? You think the pigs will think clearly when the shit hits the fan?

CLAY: I don't—

MAN: Look, when it happens, the sheep will scatter. They will panic. The predators will come out from underneath their slippery, moss-covered rocks and start to feed. The police won't be able to handle the situation. They're frightened enough as it is. You honestly think they'll distinguish between a law abiding citizen using a fire arm to defend property and family and a crack smoking marauder with an Uzi and a blowtorch?

CLAY: Probably not.

(A voice shouts from off stage.)

VOICE: *(O S)* Grande Soy Latte for Eugene. Tall no foam capp for Clay.

MAN: Hold that thought. I'll grab 'em. *(He exits.)*

(Lights widen, soften... We're now in the reality of a gourmet coffee house.)

(CLAY takes a deep, shaking breath.)

(The MAN re-enters. He is no longer remotely ominous. He holds two coffee drinks. His name is EUGENE.)

EUGENE: Here you go, buddy. Where was I...?

CLAY: That I'm dead meat.

EUGENE: I'm just asking questions. Pushing buttons. Probing you. That's what friends are for. And these are important questions. You're gonna have a kid. On one hand: a beautiful thing. On the other—leaves you with your soft spots hanging out for anyone to grab.

CLAY: Soft spots. My kid will be a soft spot?

EUGENE: Think about it. Something goes down, no kids, you can escape without an extra thought. You got a rugrat on your hands, you're slowed down in a big way. I mean, what happens if you're in some major traffic snarl trying to evacuate the city and you got a kid, needs medicine, screaming, crying, shitting, you got no diapers...it's a nightmare. Or bullets start to fly? You think you're gonna be combat ready worrying about Junior hanging off your woman's teat? *Please.* Let's deal with reality. Let's be adults about this.

(CLAY *takes a tentative sip of his drink. Too hot. Ouch)*

(EUGENE *studies* CLAY *in the silence.)*

(Beat)

EUGENE: So that's all I'm saying. No big deal.
(He pushes back from the table.)

CLAY: *(Soft)* What do I do?

EUGENE: Let's get back.

CLAY: What the heck am I s'posed to do?

EUGENE: I'm heading back to the veal stall, man. You ready to stroll?

CLAY: Eugene!

(That was loud. EUGENE *looks around, a tad uncomfortable.)*

EUGENE: Um, what?

CLAY: What'm I supposed to do?

EUGENE: Cover your soft spots. *(He exits.)*

(CLAY *sits there.)*

(Sounds of rioting, screaming and chaos rise as lights fade.)

Scene 2
CLAY'S HOUSE

(Living room. CLAY *watches as* TERRI *looks over some pamphlets, catalogs and floor plans.)*

TERRI: I don't...I...I'm not understanding this.

CLAY: It's what you wanted.

TERRI: Uh, okay...

CLAY: What you asked me to do.

TERRI: This?

CLAY: That's right.

TERRI: Um, "no", it's not.

CLAY: It is, Ter.

TERRI: Child-proof. "Child-proof," Clay.

CLAY: No, your words were "make the house safe for baby."

TERRI: Yes, exactly.

CLAY: And that's what this is.

TERRI: You're serious?

CLAY: Yeah.

TERRI: You can't be.

CLAY: Ter, why're you...?

TERRI: *(Overlap with "why're you")* Because this is... this is—

CLAY: It's exactly what we've discussed. Okay? That's what I'm doing.

TERRI: When I say baby-proof the house, I mean things like, oh, outlet plugs. New shelving to keep detergent and toxic stuff out of arms reach. I don't mean order a bunch of bizarre catalogs and plans to, to... *(Grabs pamphlet)* Look at this shit. This is insanity, Clay. Everything in here.

CLAY: How can you possibly think that?

TERRI: *(Grabs floor plans)* Bullet-proofed windows? "Convert upstairs study into bio-safe room." That's my office you're talking about.

CLAY: I thought you'd appreciate the gesture.

TERRI: And this here—a gun slot in the front door?

CLAY: Yeah, that's right. Big enough to stick a shotgun out.

TERRI: A *shotgun*!?

CLAY: Perfect weapon for hallway combat and crowd control.

TERRI: This is Pasadena not Rwanda.

CLAY: Not yet.

(Pause)

TERRI: You really think this's what I was talking about? Be honest.

CLAY: It's...an opportunity.

TERRI: For...?

CLAY: A chance for us to...take steps...to make us safe. You, me, and the baby.

TERRI: This is Eugene talking.

CLAY: Hon—

TERRI: Him with his paranoid theories and doomsday scenarios.

CLAY: Jesus, give me some credit.

TERRI: It's not credit I'm handing out.

CLAY: I know you've got this "Disney" vision of the world, but that's not how things are going. That's not what's out there. And when it comes, it'll be in our neighborhood too.

TERRI: What's gonna be in our neighborhood?

CLAY: It.

TERRI: Which "it"?

CLAY: *Take your pick. (Beat)* Terrorism.
A ten-point-nine earthquake.
Riots.
Economic collapse.
Dirty bombs.
Briefcase nukes.
Small Pox crop dusters flying over Dodger Stadium.
(Beat) There are hairline fractures everywhere. And for reasons I don't get, you think there's something wrong because I see them. You should thank me.

TERRI: For living in fear?

CLAY: For having vision. Taking action for all the right reasons. When you've got a family, that's called being responsible.

(Pause)

TERRI: How are the headaches?

(CLAY laughs.)

TERRI: What?

CLAY: That's what you think this's about?

TERRI: Well, have you?

CLAY: Yes. So?

TERRI: Forget it.

CLAY: No, I wanna know. You think this's about 9-11?

TERRI: Don't call it that.

CLAY: Why not?

TERRI: Just, please...don't.

CLAY: It was *my* 9-11.

TERRI: Clay, there is only, and will only ever be, one 9-11. A very big event.

CLAY: Mine was big enough for me. September 11, *2006.*

TERRI: It's a perversion to equate the two and really, especially in front of other people, I wish you wouldn't.

CLAY: Was I almost killed?

TERRI: Clay...

CLAY: Was I? Did I make it up? Did I make up this scar?

TERRI: You can barely see it.

CLAY: And so, what's that's s'posed to mean?

TERRI: Nothing. Forget it.

CLAY: Terri—

TERRI: You had a fucked-up thing happen. I know that, but—

CLAY: There are threats out there. Dangerous threats. From Mad Cow to mega-droughts—

TERRI: Jesus, please!

CLAY: Yeah, laugh. That's the correct response. Laugh all you want. But our son is gonna have a very different world to live in than the one we've had most of our lives. So chuckle, go ahead.

TERRI: You know, maybe...just maybe...I'd take these concerns of yours more seriously, but...

CLAY: But what? *(Beat)* Tell me: But what?

TERRI: You can't even stop that jerk from letting his dog crap on our lawn. *(Beat)*

CLAY: What d'you mean?

TERRI: I think you know.

(Pause)

*(*CLAY *tries to keep the sound of dread from showing in his voice.)*

CLAY: It...happened again?

TERRI: Every morning. Every morning I go out to get the paper, there it is...a little brown stack just... steaming there.

CLAY: But I put a sign up.

TERRI: Yes, well, apparently "please curb your dog" is not an effective deterrent. *(Beat)* So! Why don't we start with the dog poop, and if you handle that, we can work our way up to dirty bombs, killer asteroids and the end of civilization. Okay? Do we have a deal?

*(*CLAY *goes to the window. Stares out at his lawn)*

TERRI: I'm sorry. I know...I know how I get. It's just... We need to stay focused. We both have to be better... better than we've been in the past. It's not about just us anymore. Or our fear. Bad things happen. You get into a fender-bender and some prick attacks you. That's not an indictment of who you are. *(Beat)* Hey. Look at me. We're gonna be good parents. *(Beat)* Can we just... try...try our best to...keep things in perspective?

*(*CLAY *doesn't answer.)*

(A few long moments)

(The phone rings.)

*(*CLAY *doesn't move from the window.)*

(TERRI *grabs the phone off the cradle.*)

TERRI: Hello? Who is...Ray? Is this...Ray? Yeah... Just... hold on...

CLAY: I'll call back tomorrow.

TERRI: (*Cover receiver*) No. You need to take this. Now.

(*A separate pool of light rises on* CLAY's *brother,* RAY, *thirty-eight. He's at a pay phone on some dark street corner.*)

(RAY *has no pants on. He's wearing cowboy boots, a Kiss T-shirt, and a pair of filthy bun-huggers. He talks between choking sobs, clutches the receiver like it's the only thing keeping him afloat.*)

RAY: (*Through his tears*) Little B?

CLAY: Ray?

RAY: Hey...

CLAY: Ray, what—

RAY: It's me.

CLAY: What's going—

RAY: They did it.

CLAY: Where are you?

RAY: Fucking *assholes.*

CLAY: You alright?

RAY: It was a fuckin' uprising, man. They turned on me!

CLAY: Who did?

RAY: Ziggy! Deak! Doctor Figg! Back-stabbing scumbagdickfuckers!

CLAY: Slow down. Where are you?

RAY: God, I dunno...doesn't matter... (*Shouts at passing cars/pedestrians*) SOMEBODY KILL ME, PLEASE!

CLAY: Stop that!

RAY: SHOOT ME IN THE HEAD!!!

CLAY: Ray!

RAY: *(Back into phone)* I think...

CLAY: What's happ...?

RAY: ...think I'm drunk...

CLAY: Ray, pull yourself...

RAY: ...and my head hurts...

CLAY: Pull yourself together...

RAY: ...somebody punched me...and I may've ingested some narcotics...

CLAY: Ray! Take a breath, communicate to me...

RAY: *(Takes a long shaking breath)* They're afraid of what I got hanging between the legs. They fear the size, shape and girth of my artistic cock! That's what it's really fucking about! They can't drop Scrotus from the label! We were this close to breaking out! ...SCROTUS LIVES! *(He lets the phone drop and starts ranting at unseen passing cars and perhaps a pedestrian or two. To the street)* SCROTUS LIVES, MOTHERFUCKERS!

CLAY: Ray??

RAY: YAAAAAARRRRRRGGGGGGGGGGGUH!

CLAY: Ray!! *(To* TERRI*)* He's being attacked!

*(*RAY *staggers back to the phone.)*

RAY: Little B?

CLAY: What was that?

RAY: Just venting. Feel better now. Kinda.

CLAY: Y'gotta stop with the booze...

RAY: Remember that movie? That Japanese flick with the two giant monsters? Big giant hairy monster guys. One was green, other was brown. On, like, every Saturday afternoon.

CLAY: War of the Gargantuas.

RAY: *(Still tearful)* I'm the Green Gargantua. The one nobody likes. The evil one. The bad boy. You're the Brown Gargantua. The one everyone loves. The one that saves the day. *(Makes loud, weird, beastly cry, a la the Gargantuas:)* "Chur!" "Chur!"

CLAY: Don't do that in my ear!

RAY: It's the cry of the gargantua. Their plaintive wail. Remember? When they fight, they make that noise. Cuz they're mad as hell.

CLAY: I'm coming to get you. Figure out where you are.

RAY: Hold on. *(Looks around)* I think I'm near Fifth and Spring.

CLAY: Okay. Um. I'll meet you at the Taco House on Hill Street. You know it?

RAY: Yeah. Across from Angel's Flight. That works. Great carnitas.

CLAY: Half hour.

RAY: Okay. Wait!

CLAY: What?

RAY: Better make it an hour. It'll take me that long to find some pants.

(CLAY hangs up. RAY disappears. TERRI looks concerned.)

CLAY: Ray's outta sorts.

TERRI: Again.

CLAY: Yap.

TERRI: Gonna ask for money.

CLAY: He got dropped from the label.

TERRI: What label? They were handing out C Ds on Melrose. Selling crap from their trunk.

CLAY: Be cool.

TERRI: Maybe this'll make him clean his act up. Get his life together.

CLAY: He's feeling like shit.

TERRI: Listen: Don't loan him any money.

CLAY: Do I give you this kind of grief about Lucy?

TERRI: My sis doesn't treat me like a human A T M. She's a responsible adult with a house and—

CLAY: Whatever.

TERRI: And he can't stay here.

CLAY: Did I ask if he could?

TERRI: I'm saying after last time? The "brown towel" incident?

CLAY: Never proven.

TERRI: Because you won't let me confront him on it!

CLAY: That band, literally, was his whole life.

TERRI: Yes. "Scrotus". Like just having Kiss in the world isn't enough, we need a Kiss tribute band.

CLAY: They're not a tribute band. Where's my jacket?

TERRI: Give him some brotherly counseling.

CLAY: You've made your point: my brother's a fuck-up and he needs to keep away.

TERRI: That wasn't my point.

(CLAY *stops and gives her a look.*)

TERRI: Alright, alright. It is my point. Close enough, at least. Whatever. *(Beat)* It's been a long night. I'm sorry. Just...everything.

(She manages a conciliatory smile. He walks over, gives her a quick kiss.)

CLAY: Back soon.

(CLAY *exits as lights shift.)*

Scene 3
TACO HOUSE

(Night. CLAY *and* RAY *sit at an outdoor food table.* RAY's *managed to procure a grubby pair of pants.)*

RAY: Just like a job with a title. An important title that kinda says to people, "Hey, this guy's human." An office would be cool too. But the title is key.

CLAY: So, okay, that's a good starting off point. You want a job. A normal, nine-to-five job. Great.

RAY: 'Cept I got no skills. I can't do anything. I feel like totally useless. Like why didn't mom or The Bob ever make us learn something worthwhile? Force us to go to college and major in something that could earn a solid income. All this "follow your dreams" hippy shit. Lot a good that's done me. It's all clear to me now: follow your dreams and end up in downtown Los Angeles with no pants. Not fun. I shoulda stayed in the military. The Marines take care of their own. But see, the weird corrupt thing is times like right now I feel this way. But talk to me in an hour and the last thing I'll want is a joe-normal job like you and Terri got. I mean, you guys, both of you, you're office equipment. Sure, you're made of flesh, blood, bone...but you're both just human appliances. Some day computers will do what you do. Microsoft will never make a computer that can churn out an authentic, testical-vibrating drum solo. Big business will never out source songs about fucking nubile eighteen year olds. It just won't happen, Clay. *It won't.* I'm tellin' ya.

CLAY: I believe you, Ray.

RAY: So what's the answer. What the fuck do I do?

CLAY: Well, you need to find something you can stick with.

RAY: Maybe I can get my security job back. Still got the uniform.

CLAY: Try that.

RAY: Only problem, Constantine said he'd have my legs broken if I ever showed up at the home office.

CLAY: So...work for a different company.

(RAY nods vaguely.)

RAY: Think you can float me some green?

CLAY: I just bought you dinner man.

RAY: Are you serious?

(CLAY pulls out his wallet, gives RAY ten bucks.)

RAY: Kinda hoping for a little more economic assistance than this.

CLAY: I can't.

RAY: Because Terri?

CLAY: No.

RAY: Yes.

(Pause)

CLAY: Things are tight. Saving for the baby. Lots of expenses. *(Beat)* Where you gonna sleep tonight? What's the game plan?

RAY: You tell me.

(RAY *looks at his brother, waiting for him to make an offer...*)

(*Silence*)

RAY: Got a storage unit. Guess I'll crash there.

(*Beat.* RAY *looks away, still expecting* CLAY *to intervene in some way.*)

CLAY: Where is it?

RAY: Couple blocks east of Staples Center.

CLAY: I'll drive you.

RAY: Ten bucks. Two tacos. Ride to my storage unit-slash-shelter. Great.

CLAY: Don't pull your shit.

RAY: I'm not. When I pull shit, you'll know it.

CLAY: Only thing Terri or I wanna see is you happy. To find your place in the world.

RAY: My place in the world is being the red pulsating heart beat of SCROTUS!!

CLAY: You're not the Green Gargantua.

RAY: Whatever, man, whatever. (*He gets up.*)

CLAY: I'm driving you.

RAY: Nah, man. Don't sweat it. Best to Terri. (*He moves to go. Stops. Turns to* CLAY, *speaks as if this were revered poetry:*)
"Here I go again on my own.
Walking down the only road I've ever known.
Like a drifter...
I was born to walk alone."
(*With significance*) Whitesnake. (*He exits dramatically.*)

(CLAY *stares after his brother, somehow haunted by the encounter.*)

Scene 4
SIDEWALK IN FRONT OF CLAY'S HOUSE AND LAWN

(DOUG *holds an empty leash as he watches his dog off stage.* CLAY *strolls up holding a rolled up morning paper and a Venti drip.)*

CLAY: Good morning.

DOUG: Mornin'.

(Pause)

CLAY: Gonna be a nice day.

DOUG: Hope so.

(Pause)

CLAY: That your dog?

DOUG: Uh-huh.

CLAY: Kind is that?

DOUG: Heinz 57.

CLAY: Uhhh, come again?

DOUG: Mixed. Some dobbie. Maybe some Rot.

CLAY: Fine looking animal.

DOUG: Thanks.

CLAY: Good strong dog. A man's dog. *(Nods)* Not one of those sissy dogs.

DOUG: Sissy dogs?

CLAY: Yeah, you know, those small rat-things.

DOUG: Right, right...

CLAY: Can't stand those.

DOUG: Takes a certain personality, own one of them.

CLAY: Right...

(*Beat*)

CLAY: Name's Clay.

DOUG: Hey. (*Beat*) Doug.

(*Pause*)

DOUG: You got a...?

CLAY: Me? No. Not a dog owner.

DOUG: Ah.

CLAY: Always been more of a cat man.

DOUG: "Cats."

CLAY: Always owned a cat. Usually two or three. Now, just one. Don't know what happened to the other. Ran off. Got killed. Who knows...

DOUG: Happens.

CLAY: Yeah. Yeah it does.

(*Pause*)

CLAY: So, you, uh, take 'im for a walk every morning?

DOUG: More or less.

CLAY: Like to let him off the leash?

DOUG: It's good for 'em.

CLAY: ...stretches 'im out...

DOUG: Can't keep an animal imprisoned twenty-four hours a day. Get the cancer.

(CLAY *nods knowingly.*)

CLAY: It's doing its business.

DOUG: Yep.

CLAY: Gonna do anything about that?

DOUG: What?

CLAY: Your dog...

DOUG: ...taking a dump?

CLAY: Yeah.

DOUG: What'm I supposed to do?

CLAY: That's someone's yard.

DOUG: Your point?

CLAY: Maybe the owners don't wanna come out an' find dog shit on the grass.

DOUG: Sure they don't mind.

CLAY: You know what? I'm pretty darn certain they do. 'Fact, I'm positive.

(A moment)

DOUG: Nice lawn.

CLAY: I'd appreciate it if you'd keep him off it. I mean, I got the sign, I don't know what else...

DOUG: You can't be serious.

CLAY: I'm asking you as a neighbor... *(Then)* C'mon, does it have to be like this? I mean, I'm just—basic courtesy...I feel I'm being reasonable here and you're just not—or you won't, but—

DOUG: The dog can duke where it wants, when it wants. I can't control it.

CLAY: There's a leash law—

DOUG: Look, I'm not gonna get into this with you. What can I say? I let him out of the house and follow him around. He always comes to your lawn. Something about it he likes. Take it as a complement.

CLAY: Either handle this or...

DOUG: Or?

CLAY: Yeah.

DOUG: Or, *what*?

CLAY: I will. Handle it. Me.

DOUG: How exactly'll you do that? *(Beat)* I'm curious. How will you "handle" this?

CLAY: That's, ah, irrelevant. Because you're gonna be cool. We're adults. Part of the same community and we're resolving this like adults.

DOUG: Well, let me tell you, neighbor to neighbor. You so much as touch that animal, there will be consequences.

CLAY: You really have a problem. You're really out there.

DOUG: Yes. I am. I'm "out there". Have a great day. *(Looks off stage)* Come on Biscuit! C'mon, fella! *(He exits.)*

(We hear Biscuit barking.)

(CLAY stands there as lights fade.)

Scene 5
BEDROOM

(Night. CLAY and TERRI in bed)

(Barking)

(CLAY stirs. Sits up)

(More barking. But strange. Not totally dog-like. And not in the distance either)

(Close)

(In the house)

CLAY: You hear that? Ter?

(TERRI doesn't move.)

(CLAY reaches under the bed, grabs a flashlight and slips out of bed.)

(TERRI and the bed disappear.)

(CLAY searches the darkness.)

(The dog barking is louder...turns to growls.)

CLAY: Get outta here!

(A noise)

(CLAY turns, his flashlight beam captures DOUG. He holds a leash. At the end of the leash is RAY on all fours, behaving like a vicious dog. Growling)

CLAY: What the fuck...? Ray?? What...?

(RAY strains to get at CLAY. DOUG smiles a strange, evil smile, holds RAY back for a moment or two...)

DOUG: The Dogs of War are hungry. Are you ready?

(DOUG releases the RAY-Dog...RAY-Dog runs at CLAY—)

(CLAY *shrieks and staggers back.* RAY-*Dog leaps and dives on* CLAY...)

(*Lights fade as the* RAY-*Dog mauls* CLAY.)

Scene 6
CLAY'S HOUSE

(*Next morning*)

(CLAY *slumped in the breakfast nook drinking a beer. He looks like shit.*)

(TERRI *enters.*)

TERRI: How long've you been up?

CLAY: I dunno. A while. (*He takes a sip, doesn't make eye-contact.*)

TERRI: Okay. Um, so is the plan to knock a few back before work? (*No response*) It's little early.

CLAY: True. But, see, thing is, this micro-brewed stuff is just...excellent.

TERRI: (*Reaches for the beer*) Gimme that.

CLAY: (*Pulls away*) Leave me be...

TERRI: Clay, what's going on?

(CLAY *takes a drink. Beat*)

CLAY: By the year 2015 there'll be seventy-eight million Boomers hitting retirement age.

TERRI: Did you talk to the dog-guy?

CLAY: Any idea what that means?

TERRI: Clay, please... Did you have a run-in with—

CLAY: Social Security can't handle it. The money isn't there, Terri. They'll be thrown out on the streets. Can you imagine it? Mobs of feral geriatrics running rampant. Ambushing food trucks using sharpened walking canes. The four horsemen of the apocalypse are gonna arrive driving Rascals. *(He lets out a pathetic drunken giggle at the absurd image.)*

TERRI: Did you talk to him?

CLAY: *(Nods)* His name is Doug. We had a summit. A dog shit summit. We failed to reach an accord.

TERRI: Great.

CLAY: I followed him. I know where he lives.

TERRI: Okay.

CLAY: Has a beautiful lawn. Immaculate, really. Probably hires someone to...

TERRI: ...uh-huh...

(CLAY reaches down under his chair, puts a plastic bag full of...something...on the table.)

TERRI: What's that?

CLAY: I'm going to retaliate.

TERRI: Oh...my God...*Clay*...?

CLAY: The arms race has begun.

TERRI: That's...

CLAY: Yep.

TERRI: ...it's...?

CLAY: Three pounds of pure, uncut American dogshit.

TERRI: What're you doing...?

CLAY: Spent most of the night collecting it. Scouring the neighborhood. Piece by gooey piece.

TERRI: I can't...Clay?

CLAY: I'm going to smear it on his windows. On his car. On his walkway. On his mailbox. On his lawn gnome. Everywhere. I'm striking back against a Great Evil.

(Pause)

TERRI: What is this? Your idea of dealing with the situation? Getting arrested? Humiliating yourself. What kind of thinking is this? Where does it come from?

CLAY: Instinct. I just look at our every day world... the challenges...

TERRI: I'm not following.

(A long pause)

CLAY: Think about it...if things went bad, if society descends into madness—we're just a few catastrophic events away from being Planet Darfur—I mean, look at New Orleans. The shit that went down in the Super Dome. This asshole with the dog is the same kind of guy who'll be marauding through the neighborhood trying to take our things...raping and pillaging. But what am I supposed to do? Hit him? Then what? Let him sue me? Huh? What if I go to jail? And jail... the people there... There are so many factors...things that could go wrong...

TERRI: Anything ever did go wrong, we could handle it.

CLAY: Sure.

TERRI: It's the only way to live. The only sane way to face the world.

CLAY: What you said before. About being better than we are. Than we've been. For the baby. You're right. I can't be weak. I've been weak...but...I have to be strong. I can be.

TERRI: I know you can.

(Pause)

CLAY: *(Checks watch)* I'm gonna be late again.

TERRI: Can't go in the way you are. Eugene can pick up the slack for once.

CLAY: I'll be fine.

TERRI: With beer on your breath?

CLAY: I'm going in.

TERRI: Then I'm getting some coffee started...

(CLAY shrugs "okay".)

(TERRI exits. CLAY rises to his feet, doesn't seem that steady. Talks to her in the other room.)

CLAY: There's a co-worker of mine. I see him, usually, in the mornings, sometimes we share an elevator. *(Beat)* This guy has no hands. Just metal claw-things. He has a limp. His face is deformed. I was told it was some kind of boating accident when he was a kid, caught in the propellers. Someone else said he was born that way. A horrific birth defect. *(Beat)* But this man, this human monstrosity, who has no real hope for love or a normal life, this man attacks his day with enthusiasm and vigor. Always a smile...actually, his face as it is, I'm not sure if what he does is a smile, but it feels like one... it's a grimace really—the point is he seems absolutely robust in the morning, taking on what must be daily, mind-boggling obstacles. After I see him, I'm always able to reflect on the life we've got...thankful for small things...the fact I've got hands and a working face. *(Beat)* But that doesn't last long. That feeling. The effect he has. Maybe I should invite him to live with us. Keep him around. We could pay his medical bills, whatever kind of therapy he gets...we could carpool to work together...he'd be this constant source of strength. Like a spiritual pet. *(Beat)* That's what I need. *(He mulls this bizarre idea.)* A spiritual pet.

Scene 7
AN OFFICE

(CLAY *stands there clutching his briefcase, a sack lunch and a cup of Starbucks.*)

(EUGENE *slumped behind the desk. His hair is a mess. His tie is loose.*)

EUGENE: Thought my thirties were gonna be great. Now? Here I am. Here we are. And it sucks majorly. Am I right?

CLAY: You slept in my office again, didn't you?

EUGENE: (*Shows the top of his head*) Do you see this? Game over. I tell yah, chicks think they got problems, try balding. Think they could stand up to that? Can you even begin to picture Halle Berry with a huge bald-spot? Angelina Jolie with thinning hair? J-Lo with a comb-over? I mean, c'mon, it's cruel. Goddamn cruel.

CLAY: Can I sit in my chair?

EUGENE: Whatever you do, don't leave Terri.

CLAY: Please?

(EUGENE *gets up...his shirt is untucked.*)

EUGENE: She's a good woman. A damn good woman.

CLAY: I know.

EUGENE: But I'm saying: Don't do it. You're lucky to have her.

(CLAY *puts his stuff down, tries to settle in.*)

EUGENE: And if you do, if you ever decide you're gonna do something stupid like me? Meditate first.

CLAY: Since when do you...?

EUGENE: I'm saying...if I did. *If I did,* maybe this wouldn't've happened.

CLAY: Still not following.

EUGENE: If I had done some guided meditation— and I'm not talking, like, "om" shit. I'm saying, if I'd spent time visualizing the *consequences* of my actions...

CLAY: Which are?

(EUGENE *stares off, perhaps trying to find the right words.*)

EUGENE: You have to visualize her fucking another guy. There. I said it. Like in full porn-detail. Hard X stuff. The kind you download off creepy web sites. *That's* what I'm talking about. And blowing him. That's a must. You gotta see her blowing the potential new guys. Slowly. The whole sordid boat. Because, I mean it, if you're not prepared for that...

CLAY: Oh, okay...I got it.

EUGENE: What...?

CLAY: I got it now. What this is. Liz. Liz is dating.

(EUGENE *blinks a few times. Looks away*)

CLAY: Well. Good for her. Right?

(EUGENE *shoots him a look.*)

CLAY: Isn't that...I'm not clear—isn't that what you wanted?

EUGENE: I dunno. Who knows? Who the Christ knows what anyone wants.

CLAY: You did know that if you left her she'd eventually date again, right?

EUGENE: Sure, whatever...

CLAY: *Eugene.*

EUGENE: Yeah, I guess. But, uh, it's just a lot—I mean, I saw them together. They were coming out of the Baja Fresh. She looked happy. She looked *really* happy. And hot. Happy and hot. As opposed to when we were together; frumpy and chunky, and let's be honest, kinda haggard. How does that happen? *Jesus.* You know what she looked like? Like one of those T V shows got a hold of her. *The Ugly Duckling* or whatever the hell... One of those Fox shows. *Ambush Makeover.* Something...where they give you massive reconstructive surgery, suck out pounds of fat, remove a few ribs, inject stuff into the lips and tits, then some queer fella does your hair. That's *exactly* what it looked like. An ambush-goddamn-make-over.

CLAY: Can I ask you something?

EUGENE: Sure.

CLAY: How come you don't sleep in your own office?

EUGENE: Now how would that look?

CLAY: Or even better, get a hotel room?

(Pause)

EUGENE: Why don't you talk to me?

CLAY: We talk all the time.

EUGENE: I mean real shit. Your real shit. I lay it all out for you. Something happens, I'm here showing you what I'm about. I take a gut shot, we're both rolling around in my viscera. But you. You never tell me what's going on.

CLAY: Totally not true.

EUGENE: It's 'cause of the promotion. I'm your boss and now—

CLAY: You're *not* my boss.

EUGENE: Okay, fine, *supervisor*. I'm your supervisor, now the dynamics have changed...

CLAY: Nothing's changed. You're you, I'm me. It's...

EUGENE: You sure about that?

CLAY: Positive.

(Silence)

EUGENE: Guess I'll just have to take your word for it. Hand me my watch.

(EUGENE *points to his watch on* CLAY's *desk.* CLAY *hands it to him.* EUGENE *checks it, slips it on.*)

EUGENE: Shit, I gotta bust nuts. Got a presentation with Phillips and the new Marketing creature. *(He begins to tuck his shirt in, fix his hair, etc.)*

CLAY: This guy on my street...

EUGENE: Yeah...?

CLAY: Having a little problem.

EUGENE: How so?

CLAY: He lets his dog...defecate...on my lawn.

EUGENE: Y'tell this sick prick to stop?

CLAY: *(Nods)* Told me kiss his ass.

EUGENE: Okay, hold up: That a quote?

CLAY: More or less. The gist of it.

EUGENE: That's naked goddamn aggression.

CLAY: Yeah.

EUGENE: "Yeah." *(Beat)* So what're you gonna do about it?

CLAY: Honestly...I... Just... Y'know, it's hard to, to...

EUGENE: Okay, okay...we can deal with this. I'm great at this kind of thing. *(Thinks)* Ask yourself: What would the Prez do?

CLAY: Doubt he has to worry about this kind of stuff.

EUGENE: Three words: Shock and Awe.

CLAY: I...don't follow.

EUGENE: An overwhelming show of masculine force. KABLAM!! Total devastation. Bush style.

CLAY: Explain how this translates to...?

EUGENE: Do I gotta hold your dick while you go pee? Teach this guy and his bow-wow a lesson. Defend your sovereignty.

CLAY: Eugene, c'mon...

EUGENE: What...?

CLAY: I'm asking for some honest help. You say "open up". I do, and—

EUGENE: What's your option? Let this guy bully you? Cower in your house? That's how dictators are born.

CLAY: Dictators...sure.

EUGENE: 'Member when Dubya landed on the carrier?

CLAY: "War's over"...?

EUGENE: Exactly.

CLAY: So?

EUGENE: You didn't notice the massive bulge in his flight suit? Hell, everyone did. And that's not some perverted gay thing, it's just a fact: Say what you want about his presidency, like him or hate him, Bush 43 was hung like a Tijuana mule.

CLAY: And this has what to do with...?

EUGENE: Swagger, bravado, and the intensity to back it up.

(Pause)

CLAY: This what my life's come down to?

EUGENE: Things're getting scaled back. Sure, old days you'd be pissed off at a great white whale. Stand up on a mountain top and shake your fist at God while lightning strikes all around. These days, it's a little yap-yap dog crappin' on your crab grass. Live with it.

CLAY: So I gotta go eye-ball-to-eye-ball with this guy? Shock and awe his doggie?

EUGENE: Whatever it takes.

CLAY: I'm just not sure I could do something like that. In a conflict? Follow-through? Seems over-the-top.

EUGENE: Hate to say it, maybe you thought this way a bit more, you'd be *my* supervisor.

CLAY: Thanks, Eugene. That's kind.

EUGENE: Just trying to light a fire, y'know? And while we're on the subject, I have noticed you've been drifting in just a tad late...

CLAY: Been lots of construction on Santa Monica...

EUGENE: Yeah, sure...let's put and end to it, 'kay? Leave ten minutes earlier or something. Don't wanna have to take you behind the wood shed. *(Beat)* I'm kidding. But not really. *(He now looks professional. He does a little stretch.)*

EUGENE: Think I'm good to go. You gonna be okay?

CLAY: I'm fine. Just, you know...pondering.

EUGENE: NO! No pondering. There is nothing to ponder, except maybe one thing...

CLAY: What's that?

EUGENE: Shock and awe, stud. Shock and fucking awe.

(EUGENE exits with a chuckle of self-amusement. CLAY sits there...as he zones out...the sounds of bombing thunders in the distance...)

Scene 8
CLAY'S FRONT LAWN

(Morning. The comforting sound of sprinklers in the distance)

(CLAY, wearing a bathrobe over a T-shirt, sits in a lawn chair, sipping from a 7-Eleven travel mug, eyes hard and determined as he stares off. A golf club rests next to him on the grass.)

(TERRI enters.)

TERRI: I nuked some turkey links.

CLAY: Later.

TERRI: *(Claps her hands)* Let's do it. Come on!

CLAY: In a while.

TERRI: Up you go...

CLAY: Um, Terri, I'm kinda....

TERRI: How about some chorizo? Scrambled up and—

CLAY: I don't want breakfast.

(She notices the golf club.)

TERRI: Listen: whatever you're doing; don't. Okay, let's just not. Come in.

CLAY: And let our property get desecrated again? I don't think so.

TERRI: *(Re: golf club)* That's your solution?

CLAY: Don't touch...

TERRI: Give me—

CLAY: No. Just stop.

TERRI: You gonna hit this guy? That the plan, Clay?

CLAY: *(Holds up club)* This is called a deterrence.
If he chooses to ignore it, well, he can deal with the
consequences.

TERRI: No. Uh-uh... This isn't gonna happen.

CLAY: It's already happening. Here. Now. Get in the
moment, honey.

TERRI: This isn't what you do...

CLAY: I'm not doing anything! I'm sitting on my lawn.
MY LAWN. If that makes me irrational then I don't
know what kind of world this's supposed to be.

TERRI: If the dog comes over...just call the police.

CLAY: Sure. I need the cops to handle a dog on my
lawn. That's how weak I am.

TERRI: It's how these situations get settled.

CLAY: And when there are no cops?

TERRI: Christ, don't start on that shit again!

CLAY: No, LOOK, you said I couldn't handle this.
You didn't tell me to call any cops. You said I...
I couldn't handle this. Well I'm handling it now.
(Beat) What kind of father can't stop a dog from shitting
on his family's lawn? What would my kid think?

TERRI: Let's discuss this inside.

CLAY: Sure, I'll just crawl inside so you can look down
on me...

TERRI: I don't—that's so stupid!

CLAY: You sneer at my concerns and throw this crap in
my face! So here I am! Dealing with reality.

TERRI: Look, okay, you want to fortify the house, fine. You win.

(TERRI *waits for* CLAY *to get up. He doesn't move.*)

CLAY: Ever pour salt on a slug when you were a kid?

TERRI: Of course not.

CLAY: They fizz and bubble, Ter. *(Beat)* That won't happen to me. I will not fizz, nor will I bubble.

(A dog yaps. CLAY *and* TERRI *look off stage.)*

CLAY: *(Steeling himself)* Here we go.

TERRI: Inside. Now.

CLAY: Sorry, hon. But I just can't do that.

TERRI: If you care about me...

CLAY: If I didn't care, I wouldn't be out here. *(Beat)* Don't worry. When he sees I'm locked and loaded, he's gonna lose his water. This is how you deal with cheap thugs. *(Addresses* DOUG *off stage with a wave of the golf club)* Morning, Doug. How's everything? Great. That's just fantastic. *(Beat)* I'd put Biscuit on his leash if I were you.

TERRI: *(Walks back towards house)* Okay, you've made your point...now come on...

CLAY: *(To* DOUG*)* I'm warning you.

TERRI: *(*CLAY*'s not coming. She stops.)* Shit. *(To* DOUG *off stage)* Hey, buddy, why don't you do us all a favor and just get the hell outta here? Please?

CLAY: Okay, Doug, Biscuit has entered my territory.

TERRI: This is so fucking stupid!

CLAY: I'm going to be nice and let you grab him. Grab your dog! *(Honestly shocked this guy is pushing the situation)* Why the hell are you doing this?? WHAT IS WRONG WITH YOU??

(CLAY sags with defeat, lets the club hang at his side, stunned that his "deterrence" isn't working.)

(TERRI grabs his arm.)

TERRI: Come on. We'll make a call. File a report.

(CLAY lets TERRI pull him towards the house.)

CLAY: *(To TERRI, pathetic)* What's wrong with this guy?

TERRI: I don't know...

(Near the front door, CLAY looks back, tenses when he sees what's happening.)

CLAY: He's doing it...

TERRI: No, don't look...come on...

CLAY: Oh, see, he's...he's...doing his....

(CLAY pulls away from TERRI.)

TERRI: CLAY, NO!

CLAY: *(To DOUG)* BISCUIT IS SHITTING ON MY LAWN!

TERRI: Don't!!

(TERRI tries to restrain CLAY but he shoves her to the side and charges off stage.)

CLAY: THIS CANNOT CONTINUE!!!

(TERRI watches, horrified.)

(We hear a dog's yelp cut short and the sick slap of the golf club pounding living flesh.)

Scene 9
A NEIGHBORHOOD BAR

(CLAY *has just finished relating his war story.*)

EUGENE: Wow!

CLAY: Yeah.

EUGENE: And he didn't call the cops?

CLAY: Guess not. Scooped up the dog and left.

EUGENE: You broke him. That's why he didn't run crying to the pigs. You gave him *the fear*, buddy. You faced off with the devil and you BROKE HIM! He's probably at home right now with his thumb in his mouth, curled up in the fetal position. Goddamn, man, I'm impressed. That's extreme. Hell more than that, you know what it is?

CLAY: Tell me.

EUGENE: That's *muy macho.*

CLAY: If you say that's what it is, that's what it is.

EUGENE: So walk me through it again. But slower. Dwell on the tasty stuff.

CLAY: He came by, let his animal come onto my property, I gave him a warning...

EUGENE: A shot across the bow, so to speak.

CLAY: Yeah, basically. I said move it or lose it and he didn't move it so he lost it.

EUGENE: (*Sotto*) Was it like getting laid? I hear that a lot in chat rooms. I hear killing is like getting laid.

CLAY: (*Thinks a moment*) No, nothing like that. (*He searches for the words*) It was...a complete feeling though. It was real. I can say that...it felt very...real. Like I was

part of something bigger, part of something we've all
forgotten...the ability to strike at the enemy...the ability
to stand my ground and say "this will not stand".
The ability to need something so bad the consequences
don't matter. *(Beat)* When it was over, after he left...
I stood there on the lawn...I was shaking...tremors
running through my body...I was vibrating...vibrating
with power. *(Beat)* Got some work to do with Terri,
though. She hasn't spoken to me since.

EUGENE: Just her conditioning. Deep down, chicks dig
violent men. It's primal. Bottom line: what you did
takes huge nuts and I salute you. America salutes you.
You've made this country safer.

CLAY: You said "Shock and Awe".

EUGENE: And I talk a lot of shit, too. You know this!
Eight hours a day, stuck in my office listening to Rush,
Hanity and The Factor, I get pretty amped. But not in
a kazillion years did I think you'd *brain the guy's dog.*
Osama Bin Doggie. When the apocalypse hits, I'm
heading to your house. We'll barbecue.

*(CLAY smiles to himself, basking in the glow of a man who
has faced down his fears and won.)*

CLAY: Eugene, I want you to listen to me.

EUGENE: Yes, sir.

CLAY: The world is a just and fair place. It rewards
the strong. It pisses on the weak. Before I fought it.
But now...I've turned some kind of corner. I'm ready
to lead a real life. Not a shadow life.

EUGENE: Clay Stilts, reporting for duty! I bet Terri's
gonna have triplets! All boys! You're a major stud!
Major!

CLAY: Another drink?

EUGENE: Hell yes. One more of these. I'm hitting the can. *(He gets up.)*

CLAY: Thanks Eugene. For helping me. For being a friend.

EUGENE: No problemo.

CLAY: Hell, I might actually switch teams now.

EUGENE: Uh, what are you talking about?

CLAY: On some primal level, Democrats just don't understand how to fight evil. I've been blind.

EUGENE: Amen, brotha. *(He exits.)*

(CLAY sits down and shouts to an offstage bartender.)

CLAY: Bartender! Two more!! Pronto!

(DOUG enters. CLAY freezes. DOUG sits at CLAY's table.)

(The two men stare at each other a moment.)

DOUG: You and I. *(Beat)* You. And. I.

CLAY: I don't have anything to say to you.

DOUG: *(Softly)* You fucking bastard.

CLAY: This was your fault.

DOUG: You have no idea what you've done.

CLAY: Look, things got out of control but the blame is on both of us.

DOUG: I have a brother.

CLAY: *(Flustered)* Okay, um, not sure I wanna have a conversation with you...

DOUG: He's in the Men's Colony. That's a prison near San Luis Obispo.

CLAY: Who?

DOUG: My *brother.*

CLAY: I'm gonna sit at the bar. You wanna keep this table, fine. I'm just going to —

DOUG: That dog belonged to his wife.

CLAY: Well, then, I'm sorry. Okay?

DOUG: His *dead* wife. Cancer of the lymphatic system.

CLAY: Why are you telling me this?

DOUG: She passed away while he was in the joint. Last thing he has t'remember her by. Was her favorite dog. Meant the world to her.

CLAY: Then I guess you should've taken better care of it.

DOUG: You tough now? You a tough guy?

CLAY: No. I'm just—I'm sorry about your brother, his wife, and, uh...and I hope we both can move on and—

DOUG: Don't be sorry. He's getting out next week. You have great timing.

CLAY: Ah...

DOUG: "Ah." That's right. *(Beat)* I told him what you did. *(Beat)* Told him what you did to his dead wife's dog.

CLAY: Uh-hu.

DOUG: Asked him what he intended to do about it, you know, once he gets out. Know what he said? *(Beat)* He'd handle it himself.

CLAY: I'm leaving.

DOUG: Prison life's full of tension. Thousands of disagreements between inmates every day. *(Beat)* Brother told me there're two main problem-solving methods used in prison. Two popular choices for ending conflicts: Fuck or fight.

(CLAY *gets up from the table and starts to leave.*
DOUG *grabs his arm.*)

CLAY: Hey—!

DOUG: I asked him which of those he was going to
use to deal with you. Which principal: Fuck or Fight.
Wanna know what he said?

CLAY: *(Tears his arm away)* Stay away!!

DOUG: A little of both. *(Laughs)* Hear me? A LITTLE
OF BOTH! That's what he said! In this case, payback's
not gonna be a bitch, *you are.* When you least expect it,
expect it!!

(DOUG *shoves* CLAY *aside and exits.*)

(CLAY *stands there as sounds of rioting rise. After a moment
the rioting is joined by the sound of dogs barking, thousands
of them. A moment later, the rioting and the dogs are joined
by another sound: A prison cell door slamming open.*)

(*Lights rise on the* PRISONER. *He is an angry, powerful
vision.*)

CLAY: *(A whisper)* ...Holy fuck...

(*The* PRISONER *takes a position on the stage, lurking on the
edge of* CLAY's *mind. Only* CLAY *can see him.*)

END OF ACT ONE

ACT TWO

Scene 10
SUBURBAN SECURITY SPECIALISTS

(ADAM'S office. S S S logo prominent. CLAY seated
ADAM looms.)

CLAY: I just want to feel safe in my own home. Is that
an unreasonable request?

ADAM: Not at all.

CLAY: I can't move...

ADAM: Course not.

CLAY: I just...

ADAM: Look, I understand completely. My god, pick
up the paper any morning and what are you confronted
with? A catalogue of gruesome crimes committed just
blocks away. Down the street. Next door.

CLAY: It's...it's...

ADAM: ...not your fault. *(Beat)* Listen to me: You buy
your home, a hard working American, play by the
rules, want to build a family...but we can't pick who
our neighbors are, can we? We have no control over
what could be spawning just two doors down. In
a perfect world we'd all live in gated communities.
But the world isn't perfect, is it?

CLAY: No.

ADAM: It always strikes me as a little funny when a President gets up there on T V and starts blathering about "checking aggression." Standing up to the International Bully of the Week. He puffs his chest out, sounds very in control, very in charge and tough. Like all the sudden we've got Clint Eastwood in the White House.

CLAY: Yeah...

ADAM: Thing is, if there ever was a one-on-one conflict between these world leaders, they'd be singing a different tune. If these guys actually had to do the fighting themselves, all the values and morals they spout would be out the window. Because it's all about one thing and one thing only...

CLAY: What?

ADAM: Having armies.

CLAY: Yes...

ADAM: And that, Clay, is why you've made an excellent choice in coming to Suburban Security Specialists. We're prepared to check any aggression, be it some inconsiderate neighbor parking in your space, loud music from somebody's out-of-control teenager, to more serious problems. In your case, what I think we're dealing with is basically a border skirmish.

CLAY: I never thought of it that way...

ADAM: It's our most common form of dispute, both globally and locally.

CLAY: Huh.

ADAM: Israel. Palestine. Kenya and Rwanda. Heck, the United States and Mexico. Everything is about borders. Keeping them on their side, off our side. And to do that, to do that effectively, you need an army. (Beat) We're prepared to be your army, Clay. If you'll let us.

CLAY: That's what I want. That's exactly what I need.

ADAM: I think so too.

(ADAM *hands* CLAY *a clipboard.*)

ADAM: Now, sign on the bottom line.

CLAY: What's this?

ADAM: A declaration of war.

(CLAY *looks at* ADAM. *He holds his gaze. Beat.* CLAY *looks down at the paper and signs.*)

Scene 11
CLAY'S HOUSE

(CLAY *enters the house and finds* TERRI *waiting for him.*)

TERRI: There he is, the great dog killer.

(*Beat*)

CLAY: Uh, hey...

TERRI: All hail the mighty Clay Stilts, slayer of canines!

CLAY: Okay, Ter.

TERRI: The dog butcher of Lilac Lane!

CLAY: Bad day at work?

TERRI: Great day. Staff meeting. "Hey, Terri, how's the weekend?" "Great, Beck. Hung out. Got some stuff done. Oh, and my husband killed someone's dog in cold blood. Isn't he a big stud? Doesn't that just make you wanna come over to my house and fuck him?"

CLAY: You didn't...

TERRI: Kill any others? On the way home? See a poodle in the street and swerve? Anything?

CLAY: I tried to talk, okay, last two days...you wouldn't, so—

TERRI: I'm waiting for an answer to my question.

CLAY: Which...?

TERRI: Did you kill any dogs today?

(CLAY *stares at her.*)

(*Beat*)

TERRI: I wanna know. It's important to me.

CLAY: What are you doing? Just say whatever—

TERRI: I'm curious.

CLAY: This is stupid.

TERRI: Yes. It is. Answer me.

CLAY: No.

TERRI: No what?

CLAY: I didn't kill any dogs today.

TERRI: Well, you know, the kid down the street has a rogue hamster that keeps getting loose. Maybe you should get your golf club and squash the little beast flat.

CLAY: What do you want me to do?

TERRI: Go back in time and unkill the dog.

CLAY: (*Grimly playing her game*) I can't do that.

TERRI: Then I guess I'm shit outta luck.

(*Pause*)

CLAY: How 'bout something short of time travel... that I can—

TERRI: How far gone are you? (*Beat*) What have I missed? Yeah, you've been in a weird place lately, but...

CLAY: He pushed me! He caused this!

TERRI: You killed a dog. You fucking asshole.

CLAY: It's called collateral damage.

(She's beyond words. Just stares at him)

CLAY: I didn't want it to happen. It's not what I planned.

TERRI: I didn't think you could do something like this. Ever.

CLAY: Neither did I.

(He moves towards her.)

TERRI: Don't even. *(She crosses to the table, picks up an invoice. Holds the bill up for him to see)* Know what this is?

CLAY: Yeah.

TERRI: Has your name on it. At the bottom is a very large number. Explain.

(Beat)

CLAY: It's about armies.

TERRI: How could this paper have anything to do with armies?

CLAY: This house is like our country.

TERRI: Oh?

CLAY: And countries need armies and they're going to be our army. They're gonna protect us.

TERRI: From what?

CLAY: Dark forces.

TERRI: *(Mocking)* Because there are so many "dark forces" out there trying to get us, aren't there?

CLAY: Yes, actually.

(She rips up the bill.)

CLAY: Don't—!

TERRI: It doesn't matter. Already called and cancelled. Told them we didn't need their services. Know why? Because my husband is a huge, dog-slaying stud and is quite capable of defending our home.

CLAY: I signed a contract.

TERRI: And I told them to sue my fucking ass because we're not paying. You live in the safest country on earth and I'm not putting up with this.

(*Pause*)

CLAY: You're wrong. This isn't the safest country. That would be Norway.

(TERRI *lets the shredded pieces of bill fall to the floor. She moves to exit.*)

CLAY: He threatened me. Us.

TERRI: What?

CLAY: I didn't wanna scare you...but...

TERRI: Threatened us how?

CLAY: The guy has a brother or something. Apparently the dog belonged to his brother's wife.

TERRI: We'll...I'm sure you can take him.

CLAY: He's a convict. He's getting out of jail. I think he might try something. It might be a good idea not to be going out after dark for a while. I don't wanna call it a curfew or anything...but...

(TERRI *stares at* CLAY *for a long moment.*)

CLAY: It won't be for long. Just until I get a handle on the threat. Okay? It's just common sense...

(TERRI *exits.* CLAY *left watching after her.*)

Scene 12
RAY'S STORAGE UNIT

(Some milk crates. Remnants of a drum kit. A big jug that looks to be filled with urine...his "piss jug". CLAY eyes it like it might come alive and attack him at any moment.)

(RAY watches CLAY with suspicion.)

RAY: Hell's gotten into you?

CLAY: Nothing.

RAY: So then what the fuck?

CLAY: You tell me.

RAY: 'M askin' you.

CLAY: Why's it strange I'd wanna help you get outta here?

RAY: Why's that strange...?

CLAY: You shouldn't have to live like this.

RAY: "Like this"?

CLAY: Yeah.

RAY: Didn't seem to care the other night.

CLAY: I've always been here for you.

RAY: Oh.

CLAY: *Always*, so don't start that crap.

RAY: Okay.

CLAY: I have.

RAY: Don't want me to start, fine, I won't...

CLAY: You know I have.

RAY: Whatever.

CLAY: And so what? We grow up. We start to understand the value of family.

RAY: Now I'm family. Wowzers.

CLAY: You ask for help at a time when I'm over extended and can't lend a hand, I'm Mister Asshole? Now I wanna reach out and you're biting the crap outta my fingers.

RAY: Just wanna know what the sitch is.

CLAY: Always gotta be some agenda at play.

RAY: Hey, excuse me if I need a few details before committing to a major life-style change.

CLAY: I'm offering you a chance to get outta this box. Sack-out at my place. It's not a change, it's a massive improvement.

RAY: You just don't get me do you.

CLAY: Um, no. Guess not.

(Pause)

RAY: So I come over and crash with you guys 'til I get my shit together. That's the concept. That's your plan?

CLAY: Sure.

RAY: No "sure" Clay. No fucking "sure". Yes or no?

CLAY: Yes.

RAY: And when Terri pops a tit?

CLAY: It's cool.

RAY: Is it?

CLAY: ...yeah.

RAY: See!

CLAY: What?

RAY: It's *not* cool with her. *At all.*

CLAY: It's complicated.

RAY: Think I'd move outta my choice little crib here and put up with all her uptight bullshit? And with the kid coming—she's gonna start with all those mood swings. Think I wanna be around that? That's doing me a favor? *(He goes to his piss jug, turns his back and starts to pee.)* Count me the fuck out. You having a mid-life crisis, whatever, I don't need to be involved with that noise. *(Beat)* You're not, are you?

CLAY: What?

RAY: Gettin' some on the side?

CLAY: No, Ray.

RAY: Well, consider it. As a personal favor to me. Your wife is a hellacious pain-in-the-ass and has what's known in some circles as an attitude. Bang around on her. Teach her a lesson. Chicks understand one thing: Dick Power.

CLAY: Thanks for the advice...

(Pause)

(RAY finishes pissing, shakes it off. Puts piss jug down. Approaches CLAY)

RAY: Want some crack?

CLAY: Crack?

RAY: Boom. Boom.

CLAY: No, Ray, but thanks for asking.

RAY: And that right there is your problem.

CLAY: My problem is I won't do crack?

RAY: *Mad Max III.*

CLAY: So?

RAY: Max is in the Thunderdome.

(Beat)

CLAY: *(Impatient)* And??

RAY: The whole point of the flick is that he had to move *beyond* the Thunderdome. Like, spiritually.

CLAY: And how is that my problem and what does that have to do with crack?

RAY: Because you need to move beyond the Thunderdome too. But you're no Mel Gibson. Hell, Mel Gibson isn't even Mel Gibson anymore, but that's a whole 'nother thing!

CLAY: I don't know what I'm supposed to say to that.

(Beat)

RAY: Let's just cut the shit, then. Talk to me Little B. Lay it out...

CLAY: What's the point. You're comfortable here. Don't wanna mess with your delicate ecosystem.

RAY: Didn't say I was comfortable. Said I'd never want what you have...that's a huge difference.

CLAY: My mistake...

RAY: Fine, whatever. *(Beat)* Now, this is my writing portion of the day you've interrupted, so if you don't mind, probably a fantastic time for you to split. I'm starting to concoct some rambunctious, hallucinatory, fuckin' Jim Morrison level poet-trocities in my noggin. Think it's gonna be a poem called "Brother". It's about two brothers, one is really cool, and he's making massive personal sacrifices to keep his dreams and his art alive. And the other brother, well, he's kinda pissed his life away tap-dancing for the Cosmic White Man...

CLAY: I need your help. Okay? Goddamn it. I need your help. There...I've laid it out.

(Pause)

RAY: Help.

CLAY: Yeah...

RAY: Against what?

CLAY: You still got your gun? From the security gig?

RAY: Of course. Answer my question: Against what?

(CLAY *glances up at the* PRISONER, *who has somehow moved closer to* CLAY's *reality.*)

CLAY: Threats. Violent threats. (*Beat. Starting to lose it*) I need your fucking help. Is this what you need to hear?! Help me, Ray. Please...*help me.*

RAY: Wowzers. Clay needs *my* help.... Jesus, maybe it is the end of the world.

CLAY: What do I gotta do, fucking beg???

RAY: My self-esteem's been shit lately. I've had a lot of set-backs. I'm *this* close to seriously looking into Scientology.... Let's put it this way: begging would be a fantastic place to start...

(RAY *smiles like he hasn't smiled in years as lights fade.*)

Scene 13
STARBUCKS

(DOUG *sits at a table drinking a coffee and typing into his computer. He has headphones on.*)

(TERRI *appears holding a coffee, walks by.*)

(*Stops*)

(*Looks back at the table. Stares at* DOUG)

(*She exits.*)

(*A moment passes.*)

(TERRI *enters again.*)

(She walks up to DOUG's *table and stands there.)*

TERRI: Excuse me.

*(*DOUG *doesn't hear.)*

TERRI: Hey...

(Still doesn't hear)

*(*TERRI *steps into his line of sight and aggressively waves her hand.)*

TERRI: Hello?

*(*DOUG *sees her.)*

(Slides off headphones. Wary)

(A beat. TERRI *clears here throat, now unsure how to start...)*

DOUG: What do you want?

(Pause. She takes a breath.)

TERRI: We should talk.

DOUG: Why?

(Beat)

TERRI: This has to stop.

(Beat)

DOUG: Maybe you should've stopped *him* when he was playing golf with my dog's head.

TERRI: And maybe you shouldn't've acted like an asshole.

DOUG: What's the point of this, lady? Just wanna get in my face?

TERRI: You were on our property.

DOUG: So what?

TERRI: You pushed him.

DOUG: I was walking my dog—nothing more. Okay? Nothing more than that. And for sure nothing gave him the right to do what he did.

TERRI: You were trespassing.

DOUG: Was I.

TERRI: Your dog—yes—we warned you! We asked you to stop!

DOUG: I could've called the cops.

TERRI: And we have a sign up—

DOUG: You know that, right? I could've—

TERRI: Why didn't you, then?

DOUG: Maybe I still will.

TERRI: You didn't because you know what you caused!

DOUG: You should thank me for not—

TERRI: Threatening us with your brother deserves our thanks?

(DOUG stares at her a moment, gets it, snickers.)

DOUG: Oh, I got it now...ah, that's great...

TERRI: You *are* sick. My husband's right. And let me tell you something, either of you try anything, you'll be in for a huge surprise. *(She starts to leave.)*

DOUG: I don't have a brother. Got a sister. A little sister. She could probably kick your husband's ass, but that's neither here nor there. Plus she lives in Denver, so... I think you're both safe.

TERRI: Wait. I'm not— Your brother...?

DOUG: No brother.

TERRI: You just said that to...?

DOUG: Mind-fuck. *(He chuckles again.)*

TERRI: What's going on with you?

DOUG: What do you want from me? So? Big deal.
I tell him my brother's gonna get 'em. So fucking what?
He beat my dog, bitch.

TERRI: *You* killed your dog.

DOUG: I *what*?

TERRI: You heard me.

DOUG: Whatever, lady. I don't wanna talk to you.
You or your husband...

(TERRI *moves to leave.*)

DOUG: ...And you wanna know the real truth of the
matter?

(TERRI *stops, turns.*)

DOUG: You both kinda scare me.

Scene 14
CLAY'S HOUSE

(TERRI *looks like she has a massive headache. She still holds
her Starbucks' drink.* CLAY *sits nearby.* RAY *stands. A duffle
bag on the floor next to him)*

RAY: Look: I know...I'm larger than life. There's a
magnetism about me...I literally give off this heat...
I got one of those rock star personalities that can be
hard to deal with...*I know that.* But...both of you...but
especially you Ter...letting me stay here... It means a lot.
It really does. I...jeez, my voice is shaking...gettin' all
emotional...

CLAY: Ray, it's okay...we're happy to help out...

RAY: ...I totally fuckin' appreciate it...

CLAY: A week, you're in your own place...your own actual apartment...that's great...that's the best for everyone...

RAY: Yeah...

CLAY: We're glad to help you get on your feet... Right, Ter?

(Silence)

RAY: Well, again—

TERRI: Clay, can I have a word with you?

CLAY: Now?

RAY: No, go ahead. I gotta launch a mud skud anyway.

(RAY exits to bathroom. TERRI stares at CLAY.)

CLAY: I'll talk to him. I'll— He'll behave, okay? He'll—

TERRI: He's not staying here. That's a non-negotiable impossibility.

CLAY: Ter, don't do that.

TERRI: You scheme with him—

CLAY: I didn't—

TERRI: You put me on the spot...

CLAY: Hon...

TERRI: ...Spring this on me...

CLAY: He was living in a storage unit...like a fucking animal...I...come on...

TERRI: ...I'm sorry...no...this isn't gonna work...

CLAY: He's my brother...you can't just—

TERRI: I *know* he's your brother, you don't have to keep bringing that up. Okay? Ever again. I will never forget he's your brother! That's established! *(Beat)* In case

you've forgotten, we're preparing to have a child here.
I can't be "entertaining" people, or, or—

CLAY: Nobody's asking you to "entertain" anyone.
And he's not staying that long.

TERRI: This is not the time. Period.

CLAY: Period?

TERRI: Yes.

CLAY: ...So what does that mean? I have to *choose*
between my brother and my wife?

TERRI: Yes Clay, *that's* what I'm saying!

CLAY: ...kind of shit is that?

TERRI: It's not a question of him or me.

CLAY: No?

TERRI: It's a question of...

CLAY: ...Of what?

TERRI: What kind of solution are we going to come up
with...

CLAY: Solution...

TERRI: Now, you say they're working on this apartment
he's gonna rent...

CLAY: Already signed the lease and everything. Guy
seemed cool with him.

TERRI: Fine. We'll pay for his hotel room.

CLAY: No way.

TERRI: Why not?

CLAY: That's basically saying he's not good enough to
sleep under our roof.

TERRI: There's nothing wrong with a hotel—

CLAY: He's not asking for *welfare*. It's a week. Or two. Three, the outside.

(Pause)

TERRI: This has nothing to do with Ray moving into an apartment.

CLAY: Yes, it does.

TERRI: It's the guy. Doug. You're scared. His threat.

CLAY: No.

TERRI: Just be honest with me.

CLAY: I am.

TERRI: Ray's your guard dog. He's here to protect you from the convict.

CLAY: That's dumb.

TERRI: Admit it, he can stay.

CLAY: Not playing this game with you, okay? I'm not.

TERRI: Fine. I'm going to my sister's.

CLAY: This sucks. How you are. How you do this.

TERRI: What am I doing?

CLAY: This.

TERRI: This *what*?

CLAY: Your ultimatums. Everything's a fucking ultimatum to you.

TERRI: I can pretend. Is that what you want? Should I just *pretend* so everything in the world is exactly the way you want it to be. All nice and neat and orderly and safe?

CLAY: Any opportunity to undermine me...

TERRI: That's such bullshit.

CLAY: I tip toe around all kinds of shit for you, but when it comes to my brother it's shrew time.

TERRI: Tip toe, right. Bullshit.

CLAY: Hey, I do.

TERRI: Bull*shit, bullshit, bullshit, bullshit...*

CLAY: I do!

TERRI: And I don't? My high maintenance husband. "The sky is falling." Chicken little here.

(Pause)

CLAY: Yes.

TERRI: Yes, *what...*?

CLAY: I want you to pretend. I want you to stay here, and I want you to pretend.

(From somewhere in the house, the toilet flushes.)

TERRI: I saw them.

CLAY: Who?

TERRI: Watching the house?

CLAY: Doug?

TERRI: *(Nods)* ...And his brother. They drove by in a black pick-up...slowly...like they were...casing the place.

(A long pause)

CLAY: What did he look like?

TERRI: Big. Long hair. All I could tell.

(CLAY has to sit down.)

(Pause)

TERRI: I'm sorry.

CLAY: For what?

(Pause)

TERRI: I'll be at Lucy's.

CLAY: Terri?

(RAY *enters.*)

RAY: Well, I feel about fifty pounds lighter.

TERRI: Ray?

RAY: 'Sup, Terrikins?

TERRI: You can stay as long as you want. (*She exits.*)

RAY: Trouble in paradise?

(CLAY *looks away.* RAY *just stands there.*)

(*Lights fade.*)

Scene 15
STREET

(*Night.* CLAY *and* RAY *spying on* DOUG's *house from across the street. They're crouched in the shadows near some hedges, or maybe some trash cans. The golf club is on the ground near* CLAY.)

RAY: Truth of the matter, Little B, she always rubbed me the wrong way. I'm not saying it's good she left, but—

CLAY: Ray, don't.

RAY: I'm just saying—

CLAY: I know. I know what you're saying. Don't. Just leave it alone.

RAY: She'll probably come back. Just needs some space. Total chick move. See, a chick, insidious thing about their race, they can get laid anytime. Ugliest chick on the planet can go out and within an hour be fucking without spending a dime. That's just reality.

CLAY: Whatever you're getting at, it isn't helping. She's just gonna be at her sister's. She's not leaving me. She's not out getting laid.

RAY: Just 'cause she's pregnant, doesn't mean she can't hump.

CLAY: Will you let it go?

RAY: Preggy chicks bang all the time. Ask me how I know.

CLAY: Can we stay focused here? Doug and his brother are in there right this second plotting who knows what, so for once can you just concentrate on one thing and help me out?

(Beat)

RAY: You can be hurtful, y'know that? *Hurtful.*

(A long silence)

RAY: I got a lot of pain. I been to the *dark side*, man.

CLAY: Jesus, I'm sorry, okay? And keep your voice down.

RAY: Hey, I've been shot at, *dick.* I've been in the cross-hairs. Have you? Have you once been in the cross-hairs? No. You haven't. Just sit around all day afraid. Got nothing better to do than worry about fuckin' space rocks and killer quakes. By the way, little side note: I think you have a gay agenda.

CLAY: Excuse me?

RAY: *(As if explaining the obvious)* I think you may have deep, homosexual yearnings. Somewhere, down inside, in places you don't wanna talk about...you crave dick.

CLAY: What the fuck...?

RAY: You're obsessed with prison.

CLAY: So?

RAY: You're obsessed with ending up in jail.

CLAY: Who isn't? That's normal, that's—

RAY: I'm saying only this: One plus one equals two.

(CLAY looks at his brother for a long moment, as if deciding whether to continue on with this discussion, then finally clears his throat and looks back towards DOUG's house.)

(Silence)

RAY: You're just like The Bob. *(Beat)* Hell, your farts even smell like his.

CLAY: I didn't fart.

RAY: I know. That was me. But I'm just saying you and dad are carbon copies. Right down to the stench. *(Taps CLAY's head)* Both of you locked up here! Too many wasted thoughts. That's why you're trapped in this fucking mortgage gulag and I'm out there free... roaming the concrete veldt like a true artistic predator. Sure, there's rough times...but I'm alive. You cut me I bleed, and I mean that in the good way. *(Pause)* Do you see? Embrace chaos. Embrace that which you've tried to avoid.

(Long silence. CLAY troubled, deep in thought)

CLAY: Gimme some.

RAY: Some what?

CLAY: From the other day. Boom-Boom. You still got it, right?

(RAY looks at his brother for a long moment.)

RAY: Maybe.

CLAY: Hook me up.

RAY: Now you're fucking with me.

CLAY: I want it.

RAY: Shut up.

CLAY: You just said embrace the chaos.

RAY: Well, yeah...but...

CLAY: Do you or do you not want me to move beyond the Thunderdome?

RAY: I guess...I do.

CLAY: Then give me a taste.

RAY: You're sure? 'Cause I don't think—

CLAY: YES I'M FUCKING SURE!

(Beat)

RAY: Heard and understood.

(RAY takes his drugs and pipe from his sock and gets them ready as CLAY takes a worried look around, making sure his outburst didn't draw any attention.)

We hear a car speed by.)

(Beat)

CLAY: Speed limit supposed to be twenty-five.

RAY: What...?

CLAY: ...Everyone around you drives an armor-plated SUV. They're weaving in and out of traffic, no blinker, talking on their cell phones, watching their dashboard T Vs, hauling ass at sixty-miles an hour through a residential neighborhood... Not the slightest bit of consideration for anyone else on the road. After a while you just can't putter along grinding your teeth...waiting to get pulverized.

RAY: You're funny.

CLAY: Why's that?

RAY: You already sound high. (*Hands him the drugs and the pipe*) Here. When I light under the foil, you inhale. (*He lights the drugs.*)

(CLAY *smokes it up.*)

CLAY: Oh...fuck... (*He reels.*)

(*Flashes of light in the distance. Sounds of explosions rip through the night. A massive air-strike*)

RAY: How's it feel?

CLAY: ...I'm tingling...everything's tingling...

RAY: Cool.

CLAY: And I think my dick is vibrating...yeah... it's definitely vibrating...

RAY: The vibration...is it starting to travel?

CLAY: Yeah...I feel kinda...spongy...

RAY: Spongy is good.

CLAY: I feel like a vibrating sponge...

RAY: Do ya got a half-chub?

CLAY: I'm not sure.

RAY: Crack always gives me a nice little half-chub.

(*Pause*)

CLAY: Ray?

RAY: Yeah, Little B?

CLAY: I forgot.

RAY: No worries.

CLAY: I think I get it though. (*Looking at the explosions in the distance*) I think I finally get it. We can't wait...can't wait to be attacked...it's true...the... (*Takes another hit*) ...gotta fight...we gotta stand up...when there's a threat...walk on two legs... *(Takes another hit)* ...you know that movie you like...War of the Gargantuas?

RAY: Yeah.

CLAY: You got that whole thing wrong...

RAY: How's that?

CLAY: You're not the Green Gargantua. The bad one.

RAY: No?

CLAY: That'd be me. Chur.

RAY: *(Almost laughing)* You are majorly trippin' dude. I bet we'd've gotten along more if we'd gotten wasted together back in the day. You're a good drug buddy.

CLAY: CHUR! That's the cry of the gargantuas.

RAY: Yeah, I know. Their plaintive wail.

(CLAY takes another intense hit.)

CLAY: Ready?

RAY: For what?

CLAY: Preemptive strike. In the name of justice. *(He picks up his golf club.)*

RAY: Whoa—where're you going?

CLAY: I'm not afraid. At all. And you know what...?

(RAY shakes his head.)

CLAY: It feels great. *(He steps out into the street, knocks over the trash cans.)*

RAY: Dude, what're you doing?

CLAY: *(Back to RAY)* Taking the fight to the enemy. *(He throws a trash can onto DOUG's lawn, yelling towards DOUG's house)* HEY DOUG! I know you guys are in there. You and your fucking psycho brother! The big, bad-ass prisoner! Fuck you, and fuck him! I'm ready.

I'm ready for both of you! Come on! Think I was gonna just wait for you to attack me? My wife? We're fighting here, now, on your turf and my terms! I WILL NOT FIZZ, NOR WILL I BUBBLE. You hear me? *I WILL NOT FIZZ, NOR WILL I BUBBLE!* Get out here! I'll beat you on your own lawn! LET'S ROLL, ASSHOLE! Fuck or fight! Fuck or fight!!!

(Explosions get brighter and louder as RAY *disappears.)*

(Lights shift and warp...)

Scene 16
A MURKY, BOMB-RAVAGED TERRAIN

(The stage has become a desolate war zone.)

(The PRISONER *appears, backlit against the distant explosions.)*

*(*CLAY *approaches the* PRISONER.*)*

(The PRISONER *smirks at* CLAY's *challenge, grabs a baseball bat, moves closer to* CLAY, *ready for battle.)*

(They circle each other, both looking for an opening...)

*(*CLAY *and the* PRISONER *clash...*CLAY *swinging his golf club...*PRISONER *parrying with his baseball bat and countering...explosions get louder, flashes get brighter, the stage becomes a surreal, almost dream-like battle-scape.)*

(The battle goes back and fourth, but finally, CLAY *lands a shot that sends the* PRISONER *to the ground, hard.)*

CLAY: Yeah, that's right! How'd that feel! Huh? HOW'D THAT FEEL? When you least expect it, expect it! I'm not afraid. *I AM FEARED!*

*(*RAY *appears. He's in a panic. He dives on* CLAY, *trying to pull him away from the* PRISONER.*)*

RAY: C'mon! We gotta get outta here! You fucked up!

CLAY: I'm not going anywhere.

RAY: I'm on probation, man! Let's go!

(RAY *grabs* CLAY. *A brief struggle.* CLAY *throws* RAY *to the ground.*)

CLAY: Why're you being such a pussy!? I'm *embracing* chaos!

RAY: Yeah! *TOO* much chaos! *WAY* TOO MUCH CHAOS!

CLAY: If you can't handle it, go ahead and leave. I got it from here. You've helped. I won't forget it. You're a good brother.

RAY: Clay, c'mon! This is bad.

CLAY: I SAID GO! GODDAMMIT, GO!

(RAY, *nervous and frightened, thinks about trying to convince* CLAY *some more, but finally turns and runs off into the night.*)

(*Bomb flashes and explosions slowly dissipate.*)

(CLAY, *breathing heavy, looks for the* PRISONER, *but he's gone...replaced by* DOUG *in the same position.*)

(*The world is normal again.*)

(DOUG *is bloodied. He wears a bathrobe and pajama bottoms. He cowers on his lawn as* CLAY *approaches him.*)

DOUG: ...get away...from...me...get...

(CLAY *looks at* DOUG, *then looks around, confusion in his eyes.*)

CLAY: Where'd he go?

DOUG: Who?

CLAY: ..the son-of-a-bitch—Your brother!

DOUG: ...you idiot...

CLAY: WHERE IS HE?

DOUG: ...moron...fucking moron...

CLAY: (*Looks around*) You can't hide!

DOUG: ...you...such a...such a fuck up...

CLAY: What?

DOUG: ...Didn't your wife....tell you?

CLAY: What are you talking about?

DOUG: So stupid...almost funny...

CLAY: Tell me what?

DOUG: I talked to your wife...

CLAY: TELL ME WHAT??

DOUG: I DON'T GOT A BROTHER!!!

(*Beat*)

CLAY: You—

DOUG: I told her...I FUCKING TOLD HER!

(*A dog starts to bark from inside the house. It's soft. Weak. But clear*)

CLAY: Biscuit...?

(DOUG *just looks at him, but* CLAY *sees it in his eyes.*)

CLAY: Alive...? What the fuck? I...I didn't...?

DOUG: You...shattered...you shattered his hip. Fractured his skull...he's starting...he's getting better...

(*It sinks in. Holy shit*)

(*Boom*)

(*Boom*)

(*Boom*)

(*The bombing noise is back. It's faint...but rising again.*)

CLAY: I'm...sorry....

(Boom. Boom. Boom)

DOUG: Sorry? YOU'RE SORRY?? Look at what you've done! *Look at me!*

(Boom. Boom. Boom)

CLAY: Please...I'm...I'm...

(Boom. Boom. Boom)

DOUG: *(Mocking him)* "I'm sorry! I'm sorry! I'm sorry!" *(Beat)* You're...going to jail for this asshole! JAIL! Assault! Battery! You're not...gonna have one prisoner... one convict in your ass...you're gonna have HUNDREDS!! I'm gonna make sure of that! Believe me! I'M GONNA MAKE DAMN SURE OF THAT YOU FUCKING IDIOT!

(BOOM!)

(CLAY screams, rushes DOUG and brings the golf club down on him again, and again, and again. AS HE DOES THIS, THE AIR-STRIKE EXPLOSIONS ENGULF THE SCENE...A BLINDING ONSLAUGHT OF DESTRUCTION.)

(And then, as the explosion's thunder echoes out... and our eyes adjust...)

(CLAY is there alone, holding the golf club. DOUG has vanished.)

(A long moment. Just CLAY breathing heavy. He tosses the golf club aside.)

CLAY: I'm...not weak. *(Beat)* I am not weak. *(Beat)* I'm not...

TERRI: *(Voice)* Clay...?

(CLAY spins.)

CLAY: Terri?

(TERRI *appears. Lights shift: we're outside of Lucy's house.*
TERRI, *in her bathrobe, stands on the front steps. It's the*
middle of the night.)

TERRI: What's—what's going on?

(Beat)

CLAY: I'm not weak.

TERRI: I know that. What're you doing here?

CLAY: I'm going to be a good father.

TERRI: Yes.

CLAY: Scratch that—a great father.

TERRI: No doubt about it.

CLAY: Good. *(Then, as if taken back by her agreement) Good.*

TERRI: Are you okay?

CLAY: That's not my biggest concern.

(She gives him an odd look.)

(Distracted, CLAY looks around, trying to focus himself.)

CLAY: I haven't been to your sister's since the remodel.
Nice.

(TERRI studies CLAY a moment, registering his demeanor
and look. Then she notices something...)

TERRI: There's something there...on your jacket.

CLAY: Oh. Yeah. Hey.

TERRI: What is that?

CLAY: Remnants.

TERRI: Of what?

CLAY: Fear.

(Distant sounds of chaos rise...windows breaking,
dogs barking, the pop of small arms fire.)

(Only CLAY *can see or hear it.)*

TERRI: Look—I have to apologize about something. The whole thing with the asshole and his brother? I didn't really see them. *(She waits for a response, but doesn't get one.)* I know, I shouldn't have said that. *(Beat)* Actually, I ran into him at the Starbucks. Yeah. We had a little...I don't know, confrontation? But you'll be happy to know he doesn't even have a brother. That's the good news. He was just bullshitting. Jerk. *(Breath)* Just...Ray being there...you...it pissed me off. But, okay, I was wrong. That was lame. Lame of me.

*(*CLAY *just looks at her, then moves to leave. The chaos sounds get louder.)*

TERRI: What're you doing?

CLAY: I can face it. I can handle what's going on out there.

TERRI: Where?

*(*CLAY *gives* TERRI *a look of disbelief.)*

TERRI: Answer me. Clay?

CLAY: OUT THERE! It's happening!

TERRI: What is?

CLAY: You're both gonna be fine. You and the baby.

TERRI: What...?

CLAY: I won't wait for them to strike. Hit first. Hit hard. Make it count. I love you.

(Chaos sounds louder. CLAY *retrieves his golf club from the lawn.)*

TERRI: Clay? What did you do? *(Beat)* Clay? *(Beat)* Please...you're scaring me. Respond.

(Lights fade until CLAY *is alone, isolated in a cold spear of light.)*

TERRI: *(Voice)* Clay.
Respond.
Face what?
What's happening?
Respond!
RESPOND!!

CLAY: Take your pick.

(Sounds of chaos rise...louder...louder.)

(Lights fade to black. Chaos sounds melt away...)

(...until finally, in the darkness, all we're left with is the lone barking of a harmless dog.)

END OF PLAY